SEARCHING WITH SAM WIDGES

written & doodled by Morgan Paton

CBP

SEARCHING WITH SAM WIDGES

A story for children of all ages from 1 to 101

Life is a long journey & it takes us all on a great ADVENTURE!

First published 2018
Published by GB Publishing.org

www.GBPublishing.co.uk

Artist / author website > www.mORGANICo.cOM   Instagram: @Morganico_com   Information about meditation www.TM.org

Dedicated to my dear mama Leoni for inspiring the story (by not finishing hers)

Thankyou to Ian+Faith for advice about it along the way too

+All family/friends for supportive encouragement... ☺

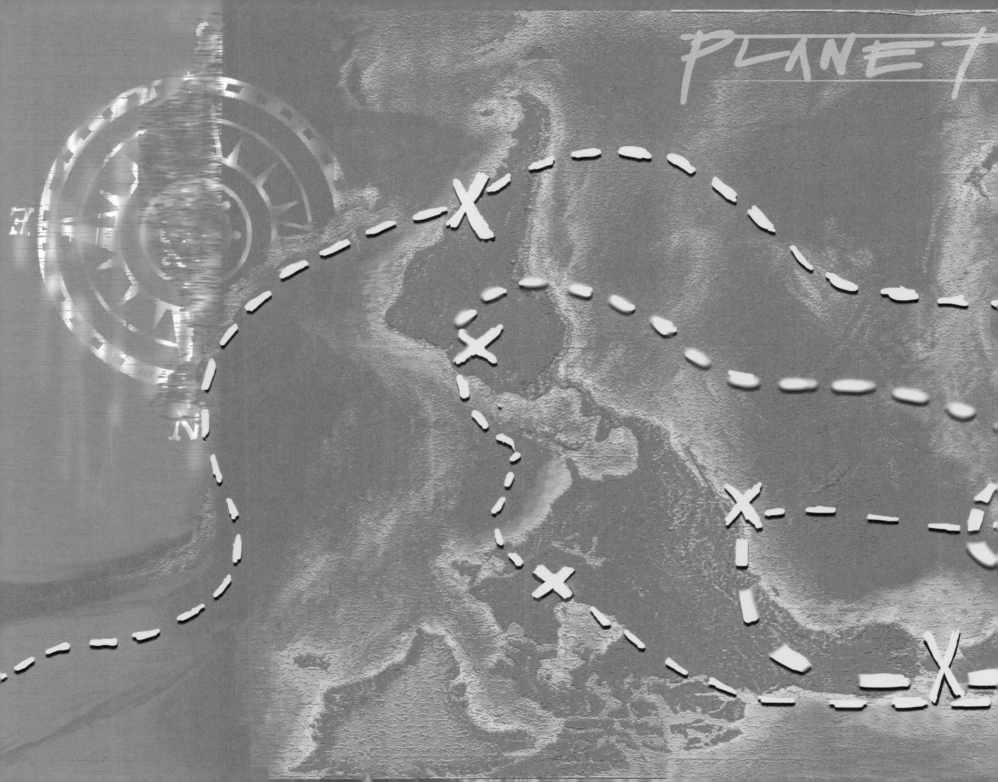

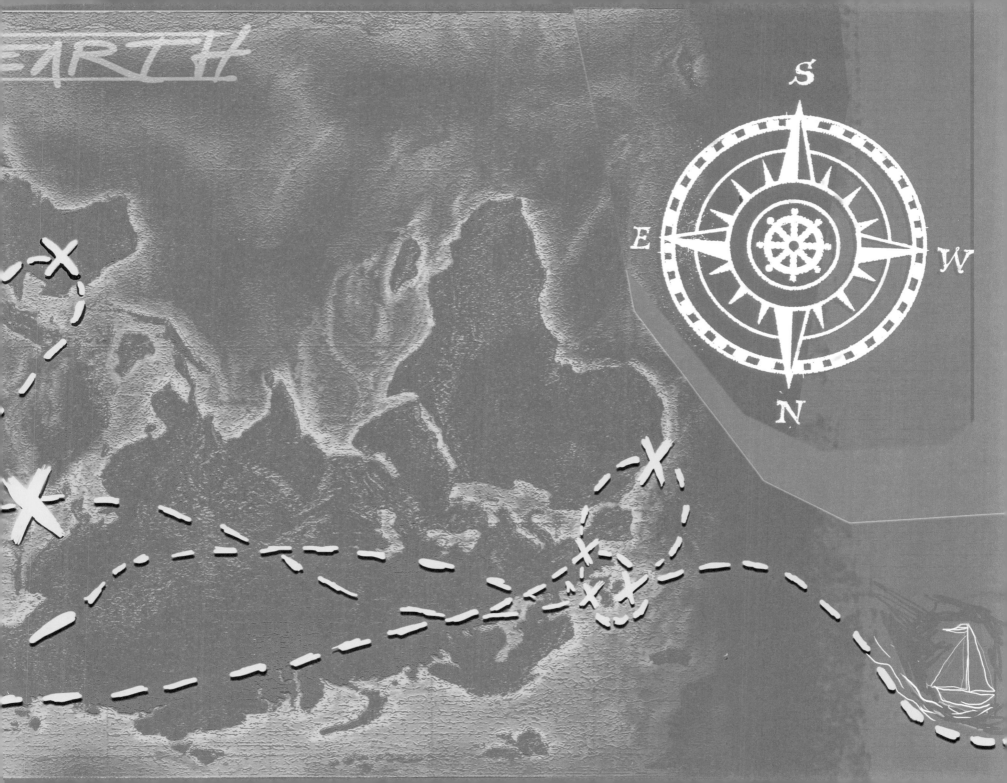

nce I went searching for something I could not describe

nd didn't yet know

ut so desperately wanted to find...

I sailed out to sea
across empty acres of open ocean
to a small, itchy island in the middle of nowhere
and met a monkey and man living on out-of-date flar

but there,

I did not find it

So I meandered to a mice filled moon
and looked under a big ball of chinese cheese
beside a chunky charred comet

But still

I did not find it

So I went to a jazzy jungle that was buzzing with bizarre bees and gazed all amazed at the ant hills, full of angry ants, next to a luxurious lazy lake

And still

I did not find it

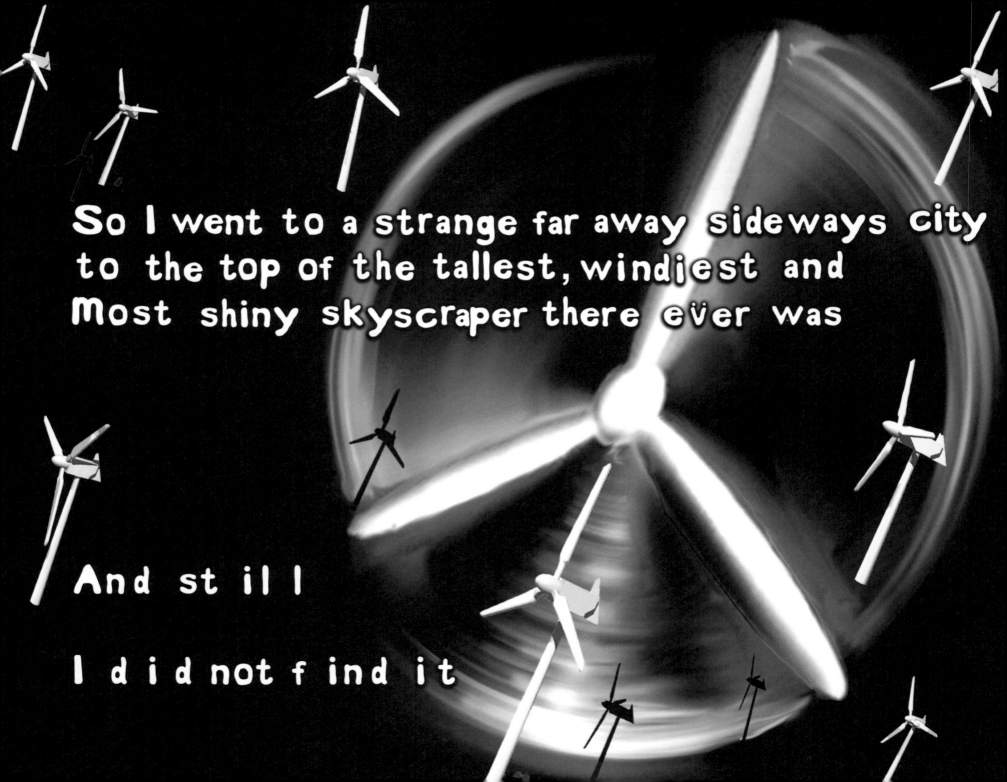

So I went to a strange far away sideways city to the top of the tallest, windiest and most shiny skyscraper there ever was

And still

I did not find it

I foraged in a fresh forest full of fancy flying fish
on the edge of a farmer's field
run by friendly French folk

AND I DID NOT FIND IT THERE either

"Non!"

I even searched in the dark and dingy dust
at the back of a bulky barred bankvault
behind a big bag of crusty copper coins

and still

I did not find it

I went to a manic market and saw a fat man in a flash car trapped in tired traffic

People in dreams were buying lots of useless things and hypnotised by diamond rings

And there

I did not find it

So searching on and on

I climbed a misty mossy mountain on the Emerald Isle
& danced until midnight with little laughing Leprechauns
who told twisty tales of magical mermaids

Of course there...

I did not find it

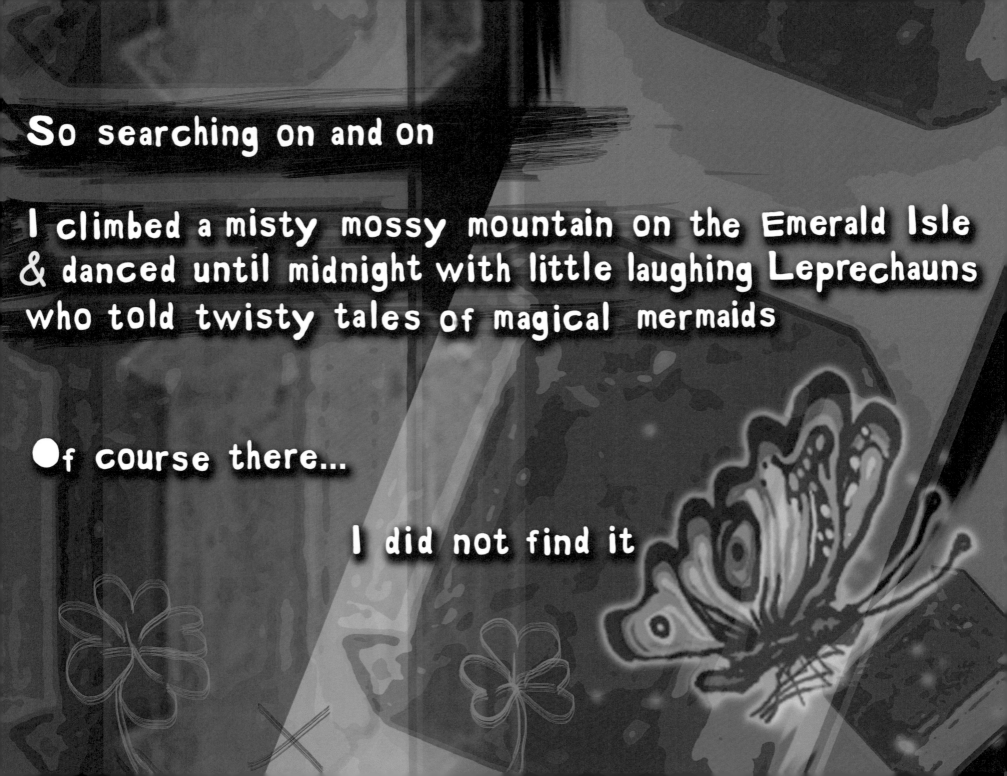

I found myself soul surfing at a sunny seaside shore where happy hummingbirds hovered in heavenly honeydew gardens

There i saw the last rare dolphin alive...

BUT STILL!

I did not find it

In a seldom-seen city street
 I sprang up into the sunny summer sky
and spoke with the kind and clever cloud people
until the cows came home

AND STILL!
I did not find it

On a sweet spring day by majestic Fuji mountain
cherry blossom floated on gentle gusts
while walking along rambling rivers
where deep dreaming fish swam
this way and that

But there it was not

Afterwards in Australia I ambled to the hot dusty desert and ate oranges with outback aboriginals singing happy history songs about the deep Dreamtime to the sound of the didgeridoo...

And all the while a soulful cooling breeze blew

But there I did not find it either...

I tried to find another place to go
but had almost enough of this crazy airplane show
Smokey metal machines constantly carving up the sky

and me searching & searching always wondering "Why...?"

BUT I knew there was maybe one more place I should
look for it...
So after having the most amazing adventure time ever
meeting all those magical people..
and after all of that exhausting searching

finding my own true self reflected back
in the eyes of everybody I met ...

I went back home
and sat right where I sat
right here and now,
in the place where I came from
and that's just exactly where i found IT....
WOW!!...WHAT A SURPRISE!

That's where it was all along!!!
and do you know what it was?.....
Well... ...

I realised..

it is what we think it is...!

We are creating our reality with our minds

(((...& we live for what we value most in life)))

The inner peace of tranquility,

the calmness of compassion,

the harmony of flow...

(((And the meditative confidence of natural joy)))

feathers..
floating on water...

Chapter 7

A lake of dreams

Gentle ripples

dreams

The End ...

Lightning Source UK Ltd.
Milton Keynes UK
UKRC031023160622
404524UK00001B/3

* 9 7 8 1 9 1 2 5 7 6 2 0 3 *